# Jazz Jennings
## Voice for LGBTQ Youth

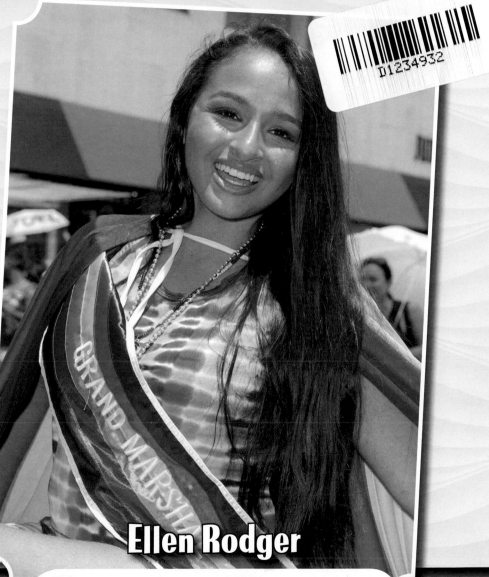

### Ellen Rodger

Crabtree Publishing Company
www.crabtreebooks.com

**REMARKABLE LIVES REVEALED**

**Author:** Ellen Rodger

**Series research and development:** Reagan Miller

**Editorial director:** Kathy Middleton

**Editor:** Crystal Sikkens

**Proofreader:** Wendy Scavuzzo

**Photo researcher:** Crystal Sikkens

**Designer and prepress technician:** Samara Parent

**Print coordinator:** Margaret Amy Salter

**Photographs:**
Alamy: ©WENN Ltd: pages 8-9

The Canadian Press Images: © AP Photo / Frazier Moore: page 16;
  © Buchan / Variety / REX / Shutterstock: pages 26-27

The Image Works: © Professional Sport / Topham: page 23

OWN: © The Oprah Winfrey Network / Courtesy Everett Collection: pages 10-11

Getty Images: © Earl Gibson III: page 14; © Lou Rocco / ABC: page 19;
  © Frederick M. Brown: pages 20-21, 28; © Andrew H. Walker: page 22; © Jason
  Kempin: page 24; © David Livingston: page 25; © Tommaso Boddi: page 29

iStockphoto: © RollingEarth: page 6

Shutterstock.com: © Helga Esteb: cover, page 4; © lev radin: title page, page 5;
  © AJP: page 12; © spatuletail: page 15; © J. Bicking: page 17; © Featureflash
  Photo Agency: page 18, 30

Wikimedia Commons: © Rhododendrites: page 13

All other images from Shutterstock

**Library and Archives Canada Cataloguing in Publication**

Rodger, Ellen, author
    Jazz Jennings : voice for LGBTQ youth / Ellen Rodger.

(Remarkable lives revealed)
Includes index.
Issued in print and electronic formats.
ISBN 978-0-7787-3419-2 (hardback).—
ISBN 978-0-7787-3423-9 (paperback).--
ISBN 978-1-4271-1918-6 (html)

    1. Jennings, Jazz--Juvenile literature.  2. Transgender youth-
-United States--Biography--Juvenile literature.  3. Transgender
people--United States--Biography--Juvenile literature.  4.
Transgenderism--Juvenile literature.  5. Human rights workers--
United States--Biography--Juvenile literature.  I. Title.

HQ77.8.J47R63 2017     j306.76'8092     C2016-907097-2
                                        C2016-907098-0

**Library of Congress Cataloging-in-Publication Data**

CIP available at the Library of Congress.

# Crabtree Publishing Company
www.crabtreebooks.com          1-800-387-7650

Printed in Canada/022017/CH20161214

**Published in Canada**
**Crabtree Publishing**
616 Welland Ave.
St. Catharines, Ontario
L2M 5V6

**Published inthe United States**
**Crabtree Publishing**
PMB 59051
350 Fifth Ave.,  59th Floor
New York, NY  10118

**Published in theUnited Kingdom**
**Crabtree Publishing**
Maritime House
Basin Road North, Hove
BN41 1WR

**Published in Australia**
**Crabtree Publishing**
3 Charles Street
Coburg North
VIC, 3058

# Contents

# Jazz's Story

Ordinary people can lead remarkable lives. Often, they do so just by being themselves. Everyone has a tale to tell, or a story to share. Some tales are of **heroic** deeds such as saving people in danger. Other stories are about seemingly simple acts, such as telling people who you really are. Jazz Jennings was born a boy, but always knew she was really a girl. She just had to let everybody else know of her identity. But that was no small **feat**.

## What Is a Biography?

A biography is the story of a person's life and experiences. We read biographies to learn about another person's life and thoughts. Biographies can be based on many sources of information. Primary sources include a person's own words or pictures. Secondary sources include friends, family, media, and research.

*Jazz has never been afraid to live her life as the girl she always knew she was.*

## Defining Herself

Jazz is **transgender**. When she was born, she was considered a boy, but that is not who she is. Jazz began acting as her true self—a girl— at a very young age. Her everyday courage and **conviction** to live life honestly have made her a role model, a rights activist, and a television personality.

**? THINK ABOUT IT**

What makes an ordinary person extraordinary? Read Jazz's story and think about the qualities that make her amazing and remarkable.

*By sharing her story, Jazz Jennings has become one of the youngest publicly known transgender figures.*

# Trapped in the Wrong Body

When babies are born, we label, or **assign**, them as female or male. We do this based on doctors' understanding of their body parts, or their visible **genitalia**. This is called their sex. Gender is not the same as sex. Gender refers to the patterns of **behavior** or other things that we think are **appropriate** for men or women to do.

*The stated and unstated rules of gender are usually determined by the society we live in. For example, in North America girls often wear skirts and dresses and boys wear pants. But in Scotland, men and boys traditionally wear a type of skirt called a kilt.*

# Gender Identity

Sex and gender may seem to be simple **categories**. But as we learn more about ourselves, these strict groups can be confusing. For example, there are more than just two options for both sex and gender. People can be born male, female, or intersexed, which means they belong to both sexes. People can also **identify**, or see themselves, as one or more genders. Gender identity is about how people think of themselves. For example, a person can be born male but think of themselves as female. They can be born female, male, or intersex, and identify themselves as all, any, or none of the genders.

*Sometimes people **express**, or show their gender identity in visible ways such as wearing clothing considered traditionally male or female.*

## Girl on the Inside

The fourth and last child of Greg and Jeanette, Jazz was born in South Florida on October 6, 2000. She was assigned, or determined to be, **biologically** a boy. Jazz knew very early on that her body on the outside did not match who she was inside. As toddler, barely able to speak, she did not like being called a "good boy." She would correct her parents with "no, good girl."

## Pronouns: She or He

When you ask, transgender people such as Jazz will tell you which pronoun they use. Jazz uses she. When you talk about, or refer to her, use Jazz or she.

> " ...I was only looking to find my place in the world. And in the world of girls, that meant pink.
>
> —Jazz Jennings, *Being Jazz* "

## Showing Who She Is

As she grew, Jazz, or Jaron, as her parents named her, started showing more interest in toys and clothing designed specifically for girls. She borrowed her older sister's shirts or jewelry, and wore them around the house. That was one way that Jazz expressed, or showed her gender. Her family got used to Jazz's preference for "girly" and glittery things. At first they thought it was a dress-up phase. When outside the home, they made Jazz wear boys, or **gender-neutral** clothing. But Jazz felt **humiliated** when wearing clothing that wasn't clearly **feminine**.

Jazz has an older sister Ari, and twin older brothers Sander and Griffen.

# Being Her Authentic Self

One day, when Jazz was about two years old, she had a dream. In the dream, a fairy with a magic wand appeared and promised to change Jazz physically into a girl. The dream made Jazz so happy, she told her mom about it. It was the first time her mom realized Jazz wasn't just going through a phase. She really was a girl.

## About Diagnosis

Jazz was diagnosed with a gender identity disorder (GID). GID, now called gender dysphoria, is a medical term. It refers to someone whose gender is different than the sex they were assigned with at birth. Many transgender people dislike the term "disorder" because it makes it seem as though there is something wrong with them.

*There is not one universal way to look or be transgender. Jazz just happens to be a girl born in a different body.*

## It's Called Transgender

It was clear that Jazz could not be forced to act like a boy when she believed she was a girl. Her mother, Jeanette, had studied counseling in university. She decided to do some research and found an expert who could help the family support Jazz. The expert, Dr. Marilyn Volker, asked Jazz a lot of questions about who she was and who she wanted to be. She told Jazz that there was nothing wrong with her. At three years old, Jazz became one of the youngest people to be officially confirmed as transgender.

" I remember feeling this overwhelming sense of relief that there was finally a word that described me—a girl who had accidentally been born into a boy's body.

—Jazz Jennings, *Being Jazz, My Life as a (Transgender) Teen.* "

## Trans Through History

The world was not very accepting of transgender people when Jazz was first identified as one in 2003. Part of that had to do with a lack of knowledge and information. Transgender people aren't new. They have always existed. Many ancient cultures had groups of people who were either transgender or intersex, and held special positions in society. Several ancient African gods were intersex. In many Native American cultures, a two-spirited person is believed to have both a masculine and a feminine spirit.

# Hijras in India and Pakistan

In India, Bangladesh, Nepal, and Pakistan, the Khwaja sira, or Hijra, are considered a third gender, not completely male or female. This is what they prefer. They have a long history going back thousands of years, and are written about in ancient Indian texts. Khwaja sira, or Hijra, live together in communities or communes. As with transgender people throughout the world, they often suffer terrible **discrimination** and abuse.

## Slow Changes

There is a shocking amount of bullying, discrimination, hate, and violence against transgender people. This is called transphobia. Transgender people have a higher rate of suicide because of the fear and hate they experience. Many are rejected by their families. Trans people, particularly women, are more at risk for assault and murder. In some, but not all countries, violence against transgender people is called a hate crime.

*Transgender people have fought hate and discrimination for a long time. The Stonewall National Monument in New York City is a National Historic Landmark. It is an important site in the fight for LGBTQ civil rights.*

# Trans-itioning

Jazz thought that once her family understood her, she could live openly as a girl. Her family struggled with the possible outcomes of Jazz living publicly as a girl. They loved Jazz and supported her, but were afraid of how other people would treat her if she openly acted as a girl. Jazz was too young to know that transgender people experience discrimination.

## ? THINK ABOUT IT

Having someone love you and support you for being who you are is important. In what ways did Jazz's parents support her in transitioning into a girl for the beginning of her school years?

Even at a young age, Jazz knew that being expected and forced to dress and act like a boy was frustrating and embarrassing.

*Jazz dressed publicly as her true self at Disney World.*

## Testing the Waters

When Jazz began preschool, her parents were able to convince the school to adjust the dress code. This allowed Jazz to wear tops that were more "girly." Slowly, Jazz began to publicly transition, or change. On her fifth birthday, her parents held a **coming out** pool party for her where everyone would see the real Jazz. This was her **debut** dressing as a girl in front of her friends. The party was followed by a family trip to Disney World, where Jazz was again free to be herself. There, among a crowd of strangers, no one noticed the little girl in pigtails and skirts.

# Schoolgirl to Activist

Today we know Jazz as a television personality and activist. But before she could advocate for others, she had to do it for herself. She also had some help along the way. As Jazz entered kindergarten, her mother Jeanette embarked on her own activist journey. She fought for Jazz's right to register as a girl at school, wear girl's clothing, and use the girl's restroom.

Jazz and her mother Jeanette often attend events together to talk about transgender issues and rights.

# Restrooms

Transgender people and their supporters believe they should use the restroom they feel most comfortable with. This usually means one that fits their gender identity, not their assigned sex. It is also safer for transgender girls and women to use women's restrooms. They face less harassment, or bullying, there and less risk of assault.

## A Person, Not a Thing

Jazz's school principal repeatedly ignored Jeanette's request for a meeting to discuss Jazz. Frustrated at being shut out, her parents approached a local newspaper to draw attention to the injustice. The paper wrote a story about their fight, but did not name the school or Jazz. This forced the school to meet with Jazz's parents, and eventually they allowed Jazz to be registered as a girl. She could also wear skirts, as long as she wore shorts underneath. The school, however, wouldn't budge on the restroom issue. Jazz had to use the unisex restroom, which had no privacy and no lock.

*Trans activists fight for basic rights, such as using the public restroom of their choice. Jazz hated using her school's unisex restroom because it wasn't private and it reinforced that she wasn't like other girls.*

## National Coming Out

The local newspaper story brought more requests for media interviews. Jazz's parents were not prepared to let their daughter and their other children be the focus of so much attention. Some news stations were already accusing the family of child abuse, for helping Jazz live as a girl. They sheltered Jazz from the hatred but eventually agreed, with Jazz's full support, to an interview.

### Jaron to Jazz

Before the interview, the family decided to keep their identity private. To do this, they decided to use the last name Jennings. Jazz was also allowed to choose a new first name for the interview. She chose Jazz from the Disney movie *Aladdin*.

*Jazz's first interview was with the famous journalist Barbara Walters on a special edition of 20/20. Walters was known to ask tough but respectful questions.*

## You're Not Alone

One reason the family agreed to the interview was because they had become involved in transgender education programs. Jazz and her family wanted other transgender kids to know that they weren't alone. The family had started a charity, The TransKids Purple Rainbow Foundation. It helps educate people about trans youth and raise money for trans kids. With the Barbara Walters interview, Jazz was now "out" to an audience of millions of people.

*Jazz and her mom Jeanette have made many appearances to help educate people about transgender issues. Here they are on the ABC television show* The View.

# A Public Coming Out

Jazz's interview brought a lot of attention to transgender issues and especially to trans kids. The TransKids Purple Rainbow Foundation began receiving hundreds of letters from trans kids and teens. Seeing Jazz and her family living peaceful, happy lives gave them hope. Many of the teens wrote of being bullied and physically abused. Unlike Jazz, they didn't have support and acceptance from family, doctors, teachers, and friends. The letters made Jazz realize she could do something. She could use her voice to speak out about transgender issues and rights. She would become Jazz Jennings, LGBTQ rights activist!

## LGBTQ

LGBTQ are the initials for Lesbian, Gay, Bisexual, Transgender, and Queer or Questioning. It is used to describe a community of people with a variety of different genders and **sexualities**.

## Still Struggling

In her new and growing role as activist, Jazz spoke to medical students or parents and kids at conferences on weekends. She told them what it was like to be a trans kid. During the week, she was an ordinary schoolgirl. Except she was one who couldn't use the restroom of her gender, or openly play soccer on a girl's team. Jazz was also dealing with school gossip, name calling, and bullying. She had the love of her family, and self-esteem, but still, the bullying and prejudice of others hurt.

> I think a lot of kids feel too scared to confront someone who is saying mean things about them. It's so important to defend yourself. Be proud about speaking back and not shying away from the situation, as long as you feel safe.
>
> — **Jazz Jennings**, *Being Jazz*

*Jazz spoke to a crowd of young people at WE Day in Los Angeles in 2016.*

# Fighting for Rights

Things are slowly changing for transgender people. There is more knowledge and acceptance than ever before. This is due, in large part, to the hard work of trans people and their **allies**. Jazz's parents fought long and hard for her rights. That fight benefited others, too.

**? THINK ABOUT IT**

Fighting for your rights isn't just about one person. How did Jazz's parents push for the rights of all transgender children in sports?

*Jazz's parents, Greg and Jeanette, and her siblings, are her greatest supporters.*

## Soccer Battle

When Jazz was eight, she was told she could no longer play soccer on a girl's team. The state soccer association felt being born a boy gave her an unfair advantage. For someone who loves soccer, this news was a terrible blow. Jazz's parents began working with **rights groups**, and also appealed to the United States Soccer Federation (USSF) to try to include transgender kids in sports. Finally, after two years, the USSF demanded the state association give Jazz a female player card. It also created a **policy** that included all transgender players, and not just Jazz!

*Renée Richards is a transgender rights pioneer. She took the United States Tennis Association to court 1977 for discrimination. Richards wanted to enter the U.S. Open women's tennis championship, but had to take a test to prove she was a woman. The New York Supreme Court ruled that the test violated her rights and was discriminatory.*

# Jazz the TV Star and Activist

Fans like to take selfies with Jazz, the television and Internet star.

Self-confidence has never been a problem for Jazz. She credits her family for helping her to know who she is and to trust her own judgment and abilities. Jazz's self-assurance makes it natural for her to speak out about her own experiences. It's these qualities that have made her a role model for many people.

## Awards and Honors

As her activism increased, Jazz started getting more speaking engagements. She has also received many awards, including a Colin Higgins Youth Courage Award at age 11. That same year, she was the subject of a documentary. In 2012, when she was 12, she started her own YouTube channel, and by 2013, Jazz had started her own business. Her company, Purple Rainbow Tails, makes rubber mermaid tails. The profits go toward transgender programs for youth.

*In 2014, Jazz published her first book, called* I Am Jazz. *Two years later, she wrote and published another book entitled* Being Jazz: My Life as a (Transgender) Teen.

## Jazz, the Television Show

What really put Jazz in the spotlight was a **reality TV** show called *I Am Jazz*. It first played on the TLC network in 2015. The series showed the ordinary life of Jazz and her family. Ordinary for Jazz means hanging out with friends, learning how to drive, and dating. It also means taking medication to prevent her from going through male **puberty**. Going through male puberty would make transitioning to a girl a lot more difficult and stressful. As adults, some trans people decide to have surgery to change their sex. Some don't and are happy as they are. It is rude and inappropriate to ask a person about their body parts.

I AM JAZZ (T

## Fighting the Hate

A lot of people love that Jazz and her family are shining a light on transgender issues. Jazz also experiences a lot of hate for being openly transgender. Some people don't understand what it means to be transgender. Or they don't accept that it is normal. Jazz believes much of the hate comes from **ignorance**. That's one reason why she does the show. Educating people is important. Unfortunately, not everyone is open to education.

*Jazz accepts the GLAAD award for outstanding reality program (I Am Jazz) in 2016.*

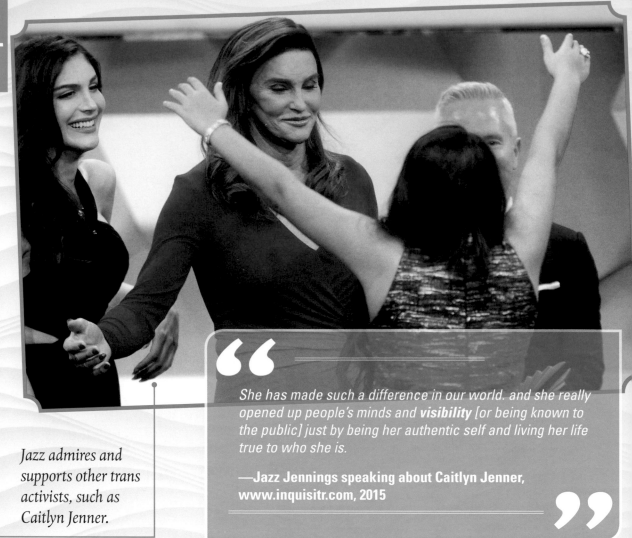

> She has made such a difference in our world. and she really opened up people's minds and **visibility** [or being known to the public] just by being her authentic self and living her life true to who she is.
>
> —Jazz Jennings speaking about Caitlyn Jenner, www.inquisitr.com, 2015

Jazz admires and supports other trans activists, such as Caitlyn Jenner.

## Just Like Everyone Else

Jazz likes to use the term "authentic self" to describe who she strives to be. Her fight to be her authentic self has inspired and helped many trans kids and adults. She and her family have been recognized for their accomplishments. Jazz even met President Barack Obama at the White House in 2015. He told her he was proud of her!

## Battling Depression

Even though she appears cheerful on TV and the Internet, Jazz does have darker moments. In 2015, she was diagnosed with **depression**, which means feeling very sad and hopeless With the help of her family and doctor, she began to feel better. Jazz understands that her roles as a television and Internet star have given her the ability to help others.

## Depression and Suicide

Trans youth experience a lot of harassment, violence, and rejection. More than 50 percent of trans youth are bullied at school. Sixty-three to 78 percent have suffered physical or sexual abuse at school. Experts believe this abuse is what contributes to thoughts of suicide and high rates of suicide attempts in trans youth.

*Jazz struggles with being a role model, but she also loves it because it supports other kids and can make their lives better.*

# Writing Prompts

1. How has Jazz's struggle brought attention to, and possibly changed, people's ideas about transgender people?

2. What have you learned about the differences between sex and gender from reading this book?

3. Jazz has become an advocate and an activist for transgender youth. Using examples from the text to support you, explain what an advocate and activist does.

4. Jazz and her family showed great courage in ordinary ways. Are there ways that you show courage?

# Learning More

## Books

*Being Jazz: My Life as a (Transgender) Teen* by Jazz Jennings. Crown Publishing, 2016.

*I Am Jazz* by Jessica Herthel and Jazz Jennings. Dial Books, 2014.

*George* by Alex Gino. Scholastic Press, 2015.

*Feeling Wrong in Your Own Body* by Jamie A. Seba and Dr. James T. Sears. Mason Crest Publishing, 2011.

*The Boy in the Dress* by David Walliams. Harper Collins Children's Books, 2008.

*When Kathy is Keith* by Wallace Wong. Xlibris, 2011.

*One in Every Crowd* by Ivan E. Coyote. Arsenal Pulp Press, 2012.

## Websites

**www.transkidspurplerainbow.org**
The website for the foundation formed by Jazz's mom. It provides information on transgender issues and news. There are also real stories by transgender youth, frequently asked questions, and a section on where to find support.

**www.transyouthequality.org**
The Trans Youth Equality Foundation is an advocacy and support organization. It is for transgender and gender non-conforming youth and their families. You can find information on trans student rights and transgender kids youth camps.

**www.gendercreativekids.ca**
This website provides information and support to transgender and gender non-conforming kids and their parents. It has a resource library and lists events.

# Glossary

**Please note: Some bold-faced words are defined in the text**

**allies** People or groups that support others and back them up

**appropriate** Suitable or proper in a circumstance

**assign** To designate or attribute something as belonging to a certain group or category

**behavior** The way a person acts

**biologically** Relating to the body

**categories** Divisions or groups of things or people that share characteristics

**coming out** To disclose or let someone know who you really are

**conviction** A firmly held opinion or belief

**debut** A person's first appearance

**discrimination** The unjust treatment of people because of their race, age, sex, or gender

**express** To show or display through behavior or words

**feat** An achievement that requires courage or strength

**feminine** Qualities, behavior, or appearance traditionally associated with women

**gender-neutral** Something suitable or common to all genders

**genitalia** Reproductive organs

**heroic** Having the characteristics of a hero, such as being brave, bold, or seemingly fearless

**humiliated** Made to feel ashamed, embarrassed, or foolish

**identify** To associate closely with something or someone

**ignorance** Lack of knowledge about something

**policy** Rules that dictate, or tell people what to do or how things are done

**puberty** A period of biological development in which adolescents or youths reach sexual maturity

**reality TV** Television shows that are supposed to show real-life situations

**rights groups** Organizations that press, or fight, for human rights

**sexualities** A person's sexual preference or orientation

**transgender** A person who does not conform or fit with the strict idea of female or male, or whose gender is different than their assigned sex

# Index